The Land
of the
Cathars

Georges SERRUS

translated by Roger DEPLEDGE

Editions Loubatières
10 *bis*, boulevard de l'Europe
31120 Portet-sur-Garonne

This publication was prepared with the kind assistance of the Centre Régional des Lettres Midi-Pyrénées.

Fanjeaux

At the beginning of the 13th century a political and religious crisis cast a tragic shadow over the South of France, threatening a civilisation then at its most creative.

The crisis is known as the Albigensian Crusade.

In the 12th and 13th centuries there spread throughout Languedoc a Christian religion, based on the New Testament and claiming to preach the true message of Christ to mankind. Catharism (as its opponents called it) would not accept that the material world of suffering and misfortune could be the work of a benevolent God.

To combat this unwelcome challenge the Catholic authorities undertook a huge military operation against the Cathar "heresy". Pope Innocent III, launching the crusade, also passed a canon law giving the heretics' property to whoever wished to take it. This was a financial and political encouragement to a religious war.

The stage was set, and the tragedy could now unfold. In twenty years the crusades (led by Simon de Mont-

fort, his son Amaury and later Louis VIII) did not manage to crush Catharism. The Inquisition was actually created for the task, and even with terror, torture and the stake, took a century to deal with this stubborn faith.

Conquering land was easier. First the viscountcies of Béziers and Carcassonne, then the county of Toulouse fell into the hands of the King of France. But resistance was firm. The feudal lords of Languedoc fought hard to defend their lands, and their freedom of conscience too, for many of them did not hide their sympathies for the Cathar faith.

Although military operations ranged from Gascony to Provence, from Agenais to Roussillon, the main centres of resistance were the fortresses of the Corbières, the Minervois, the Black Mountain and the central Pyrenees. These citadels we now know as Cathar castles remain as symbols of the fierce desire of the Southern lords to maintain their political independence and religious freedom.

3

DATES

1167 - Council of Saint Félix de Caraman.
- First four Cathar bishoprics set up in Languedoc: Toulouse, Albi, Carcassonne, Agen.

1198 - Election of Pope Innocent III, later to launch the Albigensian Crusade.

1204 - Raymond de Péreille rebuilds the castle of Montségur for the Cathars.

1206 - Dominique Guzman founds a monastery at Prouille.

1208 - Papal envoy Pierre de Castelnau murdered.

1209 - Beginning of the crusade.
- 22 July: Sack of Béziers.
- 15 August: Fall of Carcassonne, capture and dispossession of Trencavel, to the advantage of Montfort.
- September: Attack on Lastours fails.
- November: Death of Trencavel.

1210 - Torture of citizens of Bram.
- Siege and fall of Minerve, Termes and Puivert.

1211 - Lastours surrenders.
- Siege, fall and massacre of Lavaur.
- First siege of Toulouse.
- Battle of Castelnaudary.

1212 - Montfort conquers Quercy, Agenais and Comminges.
- Citizens of Toulouse appeal to Peter II of Aragon.

Quéribus

4

1213 - Languedoc lords and Toulouse consuls pay homage to Peter II of Aragon.
- September: Battle of Muret.
- Death of Peter II of Aragon.

1215 - Lateran Council. Raymond VI loses his lands and titles to Simon de Montfort.
- Order of Black Friars founded in Toulouse by Dominique Guzman.

1216 - Beginning of war of liberation.
- Beaucaire liberated.
- Death of Innocent III, election of Honorius III.
- Order of Black Friars confirmed.

1217 - Toulouse liberated by Raymond VI. Montfort besieges the city again.

1218 - Death of Simon de Montfort outside Toulouse; his son Amaury succeeds him.

1221 - Death of Dominique Guzman (canonised 1234).

1222 - Death of Raymond VI, succession of Raymond VII.

1223 - Death of Philippe Auguste, coronation of Louis VIII.

1224 - Amaury de Montfort returns defeated to Northern France, ceding his titles to the French crown.

1226 - Assembly of Cathar churches at Pieusse.
- Cathar bishopric set up in Razès.
- Louis VIII's crusade.
- Death of Louis VIII, Blanche of Castile regent.

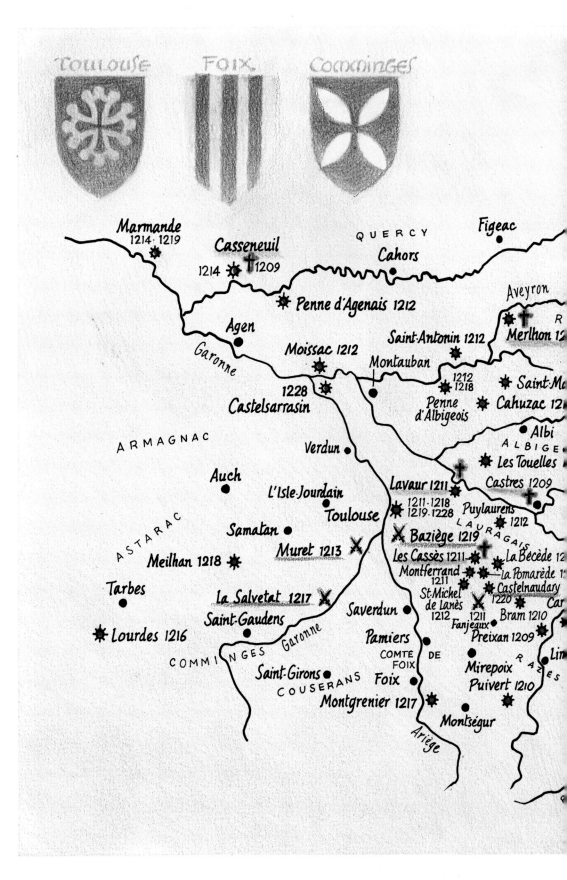

TOULOUSE FOIX COMMINGES

Marmande 1214·1219

QUERCY Figeac

Casseneuil
1214 ✝ 1209

Cahors

Aveyron

Penne d'Agenais 1212

R
Merlhon 12

Agen

Saint-Antonin 1212

Garonne

Moissac 1212

Montauban

Saint·M

1212
1218

Castelsarrasin 1228

Penne
d'Albigeois

Cahuzac 12

ARMAGNAC

Verdun

Albi
ALBIGE

Les Touelles

Auch

L'Isle-Jourdain

Lavaur 1211

Castres 1209

ASTARAC

Samatan

Toulouse

1211·1218
1219·1228

Puylaurens

1212

Meilhan 1218

Muret 1213

Bazière 1219

LAURAGAIS

Les Cassès 1211

La Bécède 12

Tarbes

La Salvetat 1217

Montferrand
1211

la Pomarède 1

Castelnaudary

Saint-Gaudens

Saverdun

St·Michel
de Lanès
1212

1220
1211

Car

Lourdes 1216

COMMINGES Garonne

Pamiers

Fanjeaux

Bram 1210

Preixan 1209

COMTE
FOIX

DE

RAZES

Lim

Saint-Girons

COUSERANS

Foix

Mirepoix

Montgrenier 1217

Puivert 1210

Ariège

Montségur

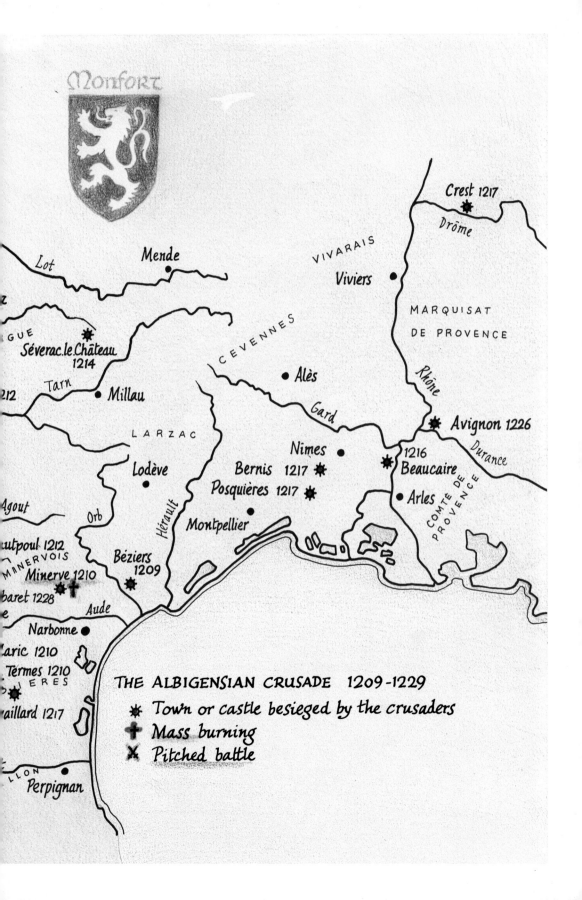

Monfort

Crest 1217

Drôme

Lot

Mende

VIVARAIS

Viviers

MARQUISAT
DE PROVENCE

GUE

Séverac.le.Château
1214

CEVENNES

Rhône

212

Tarn

Millau

Alès

Avignon 1226

Durance

LARZAC

Gard

Nimes

1216

LODÈVE

Bernis 1217

Beaucaire

Posquières 1217

Agout

Orb

Hérault

Montpellier

Arles

COMTÉ DE
PROVENCE

utpoul 1212

MINERVOIS

Béziers
1209

Minerve 1210

baret 1228

Aude

Narbonne

aric 1210

Termes 1210

IÈRES

aillard 1217

THE ALBIGENSIAN CRUSADE 1209-1229

✸ Town or castle besieged by the crusaders
✟ Mass burning
✗ Pitched battle

LLON

Perpignan

Peyrepertuse

Termes

1227 - Death of Honorius III, election of Gregory IX.

1229 - Treaty prepared in Meaux, signed in Paris, leading to the annexation of Toulouse land by the French crown.

1232 - Montségur becomes the centre of the Cathar church at the request of Guilhabert de Castres.

1235 - Uprising against the Inquisition in Toulouse, Albi, Narbonne.
- Inquisitors expelled from Toulouse.

1236 - Inquisitors return to Toulouse.

1240 - Last of the Trencavels fails to take Carcassonne.
- Fall of Peyrepertuse.

1241 - Louis IX asks Raymond VII to destroy Montségur. Reluctant siege.
- Death of Gregory IX.
- Election and death of Celestin IV.
- Holy See vacant.

1242 - Raymond VII revolts against Louis IX.
- Inquisitor Guillaume Arnaud and fellow judges murdered in Avignonet by knights from Montségur.

1243 - Raymond VII submits once more.
- Council of Béziers decides to destroy Montségur.
- Siege of Montségur begins.
- Election of Innocent IV.

1244 - Montségur surrenders.
- 16 March: 225 Perfecti burnt alive.

Bram

1245 - Cathar church dismantled; last leaders flee to Lombardy.

1249 - Death of Raymond VII of Toulouse, succeeded by Alphonse de Poitiers, brother of Louis IX.

1253 - Fall of Quéribus and Puilaurens.

1270 - Death of Alphonse de Poitiers and Jeanne de Toulouse without issue. County of Toulouse passes to French crown.

1321 - Last known Languedoc Perfectus, Guillaume Bélibaste, burnt alive at Villerouge-Termenès.

1329 - Last mass burning of Cathars in Carcassonne.

Cordes

Mirepoix

THE ALBIGENSIAN CRUSADES

Around the middle of the 12th century Raymond V, count of Toulouse, became alarmed at the spread of heresy in his lands. He informed Saint Bernard, abbot of Cîteaux. Some years before, Saint Bernard had reproached his father, Alphonse Jourdain, for lack of firmness, saying that "under his authority the area was wide open to heretics attacking Christ's flock". The heresy spread and became stronger, but it was the accession of the energetic Pope Innocent III that brought matters to a head. Soon after his election the new Pope wrote to the bishops and lords of the areas concerned, asking them to take up arms against the heretics and their protectors.

Languedoc was the object of two unsuccessful missions. Dominique Guzman did no better, for all his efforts. Leaving behind the pomp and ease of the Church, he roamed the region preaching and trying to convert, but in vain. At Prouille, not far from Fanjeaux, he set up a home for repentant Cathar women.

Lauragais

Montferrand

Dominique fought hard, but to no avail. When he realised the extent of his failure, he uttered threats which turned out to contain a dreadful prophecy. His intolerant words were recorded by one of his spiritual heirs: "For years now I have brought you words of peace, I have preached, I have implored, I have wept. But as the common people say in Spain: if a blessing will not work, then it must be the stick. Now we shall stir up princes and bishops against you, and they, alas, will call together nations and peoples, and many will perish by the sword. Towers will be destroyed, walls overturned, and you will be reduced to slavery. Thus force will prevail where gentleness has failed." But as he said these words Dominique forgot one small but essential fact: he was talking in a country with a long tradition of tolerance, and the people could barely understand, let alone accept such ideas.

THE CRUSADERS SWEEP DOWN

In January 1208 the papal envoy, Pierre de Castelnau, was murdered in mysterious circumstances. The abbot of Cîteaux, Armand Amaury, blamed Raymond VI of Toulouse for the crime. The Pope therefore asked the King of France, Philippe Auguste, to fight against the heretics in Languedoc, declaring the lands of the count of Toulouse forfeit, i.e. offering them to the first Catholic to take them, an unsubtle mixture of bribery and religion. The king, as feudal overlord of the county of Toulouse, could not accept this papal interference in French affairs, and pointed this out. After a year's negotiation, Philippe Auguste finally allowed some of his barons to launch a crusade, but would not involve royal authority.

Early in the summer of 1209 the crusading army raised in Burgundy at the request of Innocent III left Lyon under Arnaud Amaury and made its way down the Rhône valley towards the South. Raymond VI, the target of the crusade, went to meet the army at Saint-Gilles, where to avoid invasion and dispossession he took on the crusader's cross. The count of Toulouse did not play an important role in subsequent events; he rather watched passively as they unfolded. Raymond Roger Trencavel, viscount of Béziers, Carcassonne, Albi and Razès, fearful and isolated, followed his example. But the crusading clerics were not taken in a second time - they would have had no one left to fight. Trencavel's lands were declared forfeit. Plucking up courage, the young viscount made his way back to Béziers and asked the citizens to hold out while he gathered troops in Carcassonne to relieve them.

Quéribus

Roquefixade

THE SACK OF BEZIERS — THE FALL OF CARCASSONNE

Béziers

On 22 July the crusaders set up camp outside the walls of Béziers, ready for a long siege. The bishop of the town went out to parley with the besiegers and brought back their terms to the citizens. They were unacceptable. A party of men from Béziers thoughtlessly opened a gate to attempt a sortie. They were quickly forced back within the walls and followed into the town by the infantry they had provoked. Amazed by the turn of events the crusaders' cavalry followed suit. What happened next was pure butchery. Quickly seizing the town the soldiery put the people to the sword and their homes to the torch. Asked by a knight how to tell a Catholic from a heretic, the abbot Arnaud Amaury is said to have replied in the famous words: "Kill them all; the Lord will recognize his own". Within hours the town was com-

Carcassonne

pletely sacked. The total number of deaths quoted by people at the time depends on their sympathies. Modern historians agree on a likely figure of twenty thousand dead.

Spurred on by this easy and bloody victory, the crusaders reached the walls of Carcassonne a few days later and set up camp. On the morning of 3 August they attacked a village to the North of the town. Within two hours they had taken it and burnt it to the ground. The holy army had camped by the River Aude, cutting off the people of Carcassonne from their water. Next arrived the King of Aragon, Peter II, to attempt to mediate, since he was feudal overlord of the area. The terms set by Arnaud Amaury and the Northern barons were too harsh and the viscount rejected them. Peter left Carcassonne and the fighting resumed. Resistance became more and more difficult, with no hope of relief from outside. On 15 August Trencavel entered the besiegers' camp to negotiate surrender, and was treacherously taken prisoner. Leaderless, tired and hungry, Carcassonne surrendered unconditionally. On 10 November in a dungeon in the fortified city Raymond Roger Trencavel, last viscount of Carcassonne, Béziers, Albi and Razès, met his end. History records the cause of death as dysentery

After the fall of Carcassonne the canon law that Innocent III had announced at the start of the crusade came into effect. Intended to encourage feudal lords to become crusaders, it said basically that the property of heretics and their protectors was forfeit. By this law Trencavel was stripped of his titles and land. The papal envoy offered them to the first Catholic lord who wanted them. The count of Nevers refused, claiming he did not want to stay; the Duke of Burgundy also declined, as did the count of St Pol. An electoral college was set up to choose a successor to the viscount. The title went to a veteran of the Crusades to the Holy Land who had come to notice in the recent fighting: Simon de Montfort. He was an unimportant baron from the Ile de France, earl of Leicester, a town he never visited, an ambitious but deeply religious man. The new viscount embarked upon a campaign of conquest designed both to establish the power of France in the South and to stamp out the heresy. The law of forfeiture was applied with vigour, and the crusaders were rewarded with castles and land. The priests, close behind the soldiers, attacked the heresy with torture and flame. Thus Montfort took possession of the land he had been granted at Carcassonne. An ambitious man, he now turned his attention to Toulouse.

Raymond VI and the consuls of Toulouse refused to hand over the heretics in the city at the request of a delegation of clerics. They only took orders from the Pope, they said. Count and consuls were once more excommunicated. To keep the lands of Toulouse forfeit, the clerics frustrated all Raymond's attempt to lift the excommunication, and war became inevitable.

Béziers

Toulouse

In spring 1211 occurred the tragic siege of Lavaur. In spite of help sent from Toulouse, the town was stormed and taken. The result was appalling: flouting the code of chivalry Montfort decided to hang the eighty knights who had defended the town; when the gallows collapsed under the weight of their leader Aimery de Montréal, he ordered their throats to be cut. Meanwhile Dame Guiraude, lady of the castle, was thrown into a well and stoned to death, and 400 Cathars were burnt on a huge pyre.

Realising the seriousness of the situation, the consuls of Toulouse appealed to Peter II of Aragon, and Raymond VI called in the help of the lords subject to him. The whole area rose and many of the occupying garrisons Montfort had set up were massacred. Another crusade was needed to recapture what had just been lost, and war broke out again.

Lavaur

Carcassonne

THE BATTLE OF MURET

Peter II, the powerful King of Aragon, called Peter the Catholic, enjoyed considerable esteem in the Holy See, especially after his crushing victory over the Moors at the battle of Las Navas de Tolosa (1212). Peter the Catholic therefore obtained from the Pope permission to create a new state, extending his authority from South of the River Ebro as far as the Alps. In return the king was to restore civil and religious order within his lands and recognize Montfort as a subject (for the king had not been consulted over Trencavel's disgrace and replacement). Nine months after the birth of his new kingdom, Peter II had to call to order his turbulent subject the new viscount of Carcassonne who had taken up arms again against his neighbour Raymond VI, count of Toulouse. The king's duty was to restore civil order, and to police his territory.

Raising local hopes the King of Aragon brought his troops from Aragon and Catalonia to join his Languedoc subjects. The counts of Foix, Comminges and, of course, Toulouse were there too. On Thursday 12 September this army faced Montfort's, occupying the town of Muret. The balance of forces was distinctly in favour of the Languedoc-Aragon alliance, but the battle was ill managed. Careless rather than brave, the king threw himself into the fray. After a ferocious skirmish he fell mortally wounded. His Aragon soldiers brought the news to the rest of the army, and the result was panic. The only way out was the River Garonne and the boats moored there. The Northern French calvalry hunted down the stragglers and slaughtered them in numbers comparable to Béziers if the accounts are to be believed. The people of Toulouse saw their hopes vanish with their army. They had to make a new start at an even greater disadvantage than before. Montfort's position was greatly strengthened and he could now proceed to conquer the county of Toulouse.

Muret

RAYMOND VI DISPOSSESSED

By one victory after another the crusaders took possession of the area. First Quercy and Agenais submitted to the Northerners' pressure. Then came the turn of Périgord and Rouergue. Militarily it was a total success, indeed a triumph when on 30 November 1215 the Lateran Council dispossessed Raymond VI and declared Simon de Montfort count of Toulouse in his place. Only the title of marquis of Provence was left, reserved for Raymond the Younger (later Raymond VII) if he proved himself worthy.

In spring 1216 Montfort entered Toulouse, where one of his first decisions was to abolish the consuls and replace them by a more amenable body. Then he returned to Paris to pay feudal homage to King Philippe Auguste for his lands, the county of Toulouse and the viscountcy of Carcassonne-Béziers. Ignoring Aragon's claims to Trencavel's former territory, the King of France accepted Montfort's homage and with it the extension of his territory to the Mediterranean.

Until this point it had been basically a war of conquest. The religious question at the heart of the matter had been less important, but in spite of its losses the heresy was far from beaten, and continued to expand.

Seal of Raymond VI.

Seal of Raymond VII.

Carcassonne. The "siege stone" showing the attack on Toulouse during which Simon de Montfort was killed in 1218.

LIBERATION

In April 1216 Raymond VI and his son, Raymond the Younger, landed in Marseille to a warm welcome. Father and son swiftly led their army to Beaucaire and besieged the Northern French garrison in the castle. Montfort rushed to the rescue and besieged the Toulouse army in its turn. His efforts were unsuccessful, for the besieged Northerners were short of supplies, and the city of Toulouse rose against him. After a three month siege the invincible Simon de Montfort was forced to negotiate, thwarted by a youngster of nineteen. Humiliated and dishonoured, he returned to Toulouse, sacked the city and inflicting heavy fines on the citizens. After this success at Beaucaire, local hopes rose again. Toulouse looked forward to the return of its young and victorious lord. Montfort was forced to fight on all fronts. On 13 September 1217 Raymond the Younger, together with a number of feudal lords, made a triumphant entry into Toulouse, welcomed as a liberator. The citizens raised a militia and rebuilt the fortifications the Northerners had pulled down. The crusaders did all they could to recover a territory that was slipping from their grip. Montfort besieged Toulouse, which resisted and strengthened its defences. The fighting was fierce, and on 25 June 1218 Simon de Montfort fell, struck on the head by a rock. Legend has it that the machine that propelled the stone was operated by women. A great cry of relief rang out: "Montfort is dead! Montfort is dead!" they sang along the ramparts and throughout the delighted city. Amaury de Montfort took his father's place, but lacking his military skills, was forced to raise the siege. Toulouse was triumphant, and gradually won back the land that had been confiscated. The Pope, worried by the crusaders' many defeats, called on King Philippe Auguste to support them. The king allowed his son Louis to take the crusader's cross. The prince's army first sacked Marmande, then laid siege to Toulouse. The Northern French knights then went home - their "forty days service" were up. Left to his fate, Amaury de Montfort gradually lost ground and in early 1224 gave up and went home to the Ile de France.

There followed a long period of diplomatic manoeuvring. The young Louis VIII, seeing his advantage in attacking Toulouse again, informed the Holy See that he was ready to head a new crusade. The Pope, who did not want to lose the initiative, refused his blessing. Louis VIII's plans collapsed but his ambitions were unchanged. Another Council, in Bourges in November 1225, approved the royal crusade. News of this decision provoked

Avignonet

Puivert

dismay, for after fifteen years of war the exhausted South was alarmed at yet another invasion, especially led by the king himself. When the crusade set off in May 1226 the demoralised South was as good as beaten.

Yet the expected walkover got off to a very bad start. Avignon refused to give in to the royal army, which was forced to waste three months laying siege to the city. After the fall of Avignon the crusading army advanced to the border of the county of Foix. Along the route the king received the submission of the areas he crossed, but falling ill, was forced to return to Paris. The army avoided Toulouse and followed him. On 8 December 1226 Louis VIII died. The late king's cousin, Humbert de Beaujeu, was given command of the royal troops occupying the South. For more than a year he marched across the rebellious Languedoc, trying to bring it to heel but in vain. During the summer of 1228 he changed his tactics and laid waste the countryside, cutting down trees and destroying the crops. The local population were starved into negotiation.

THE TREATY OF PARIS - HUMILIATION

In January 1229 Raymond VII made his way to Meaux where the terms of a treaty were being prepared. Given the state of the country he had left behind, the count of Toulouse had a weak hand for negotiation. On 12 April 1229 in front of Notre Dame in Paris he signed the treaty, after undergoing the humiliation of a public flogging. The imposed agreement dispossessed the count of half his land. He kept the Toulouse area, Quercy, Agenais and Rouergue. His possessions beyond the Rhône and Trencavel's former lands fell to the French crown. The fortifications of Toulouse were to be dismantled, and also those of twenty-nine other strongholds. The count was to pay a considerable amount to the crown and to the Church. He undertook to track down heretics, and to establish and maintain a Catholic university in Toulouse. Furthermore his only daughter would be married to the king's brother and if she were to die without issue, the county would pass to the crown. Raymond VII was kept in Paris until his daughter Jeanne reached the Court. Some years later she married Alphonse de Poitiers, brother of Louis IX. On his return to Toulouse Raymond VII did all he could to re-marry and have a male heir, hoping that tradition would prove stronger than the treaty. He was unsuccessful and died in 1249. The county passed to Jeanne, and Alphonse de Poitiers administered it until their death in 1271. In the absence of heirs the royal domains absorbed what was left of the once powerful county of Toulouse.

Carcassonne

Montségur

THE CATHAR FAITH

Catharism was a form of Christianity; its holy book was the New Testament. God sent Christ to earth to be known by mankind and reveal to them His plan for salvation. He is a Christ who reveals, and not, as in Catholic dogma, a Christ who redeems. Only Christ's revelation can lead to eternal salvation.

Minerve

Lastours

ORIGINS

It would be mistaken to look for the origins of Catharism in Manichæanism. The ideas of a soul imprisoned in flesh, salvation by knowledge, and two opposing principles of Good and Evil, go back beyond Catharism and Manichæanism to Gnosticism. Although both faiths were strongly influenced by Gnosis, their paths later diverged. Modern opinion is that the sources of Catharism are to be found in certain features of early Christianity.

Around 950 AD a priest known as Bogomil preached this dualist faith in Bulgaria. This is the earliest reference we have. Following the trade routes the faith spread, until around the year 1000 we find traces in Champagne and Toulouse, later in Northern Italy, what is now Belgium, and even England. The most developed centres were in Bulgaria, Lombardy and Languedoc.

Peyrepertuse

Roquefixade

ORIGIN OF THE WORDS
CATHAR, PERFECTI, ALBIGENSIAN

The obvious derivation of the word Cathar is the Greek *katharos* meaning "pure". Since the name was used in a negative sense by Catholics, we may suppose the opponents of Catharism referred to "these people who claim to be pure". The word "cathar" appears for the first time in a sermon by a German monk in 1163. The medieval German word *ketter* ("heretic") comes from *katte*("cat"). In 1198 the Catholic propagandist Alain de Lille writes that they are so called from the Latin *cattus* because they are said to kiss the rear quarters of cats, in which form Lucifer appears to them. For in medieval tradition a cat is often a symbol for the Devil, and it is not surprising that the writers most involved in slandering the religion we now call Cathar should use this superstitious image. *Katharos, cattus, ketter* - it is of little consequence, for those who held this faith never used any of those names. They called themselves "believers", "Christians" or even in the case of the clergy "good Christians".

As for those we now know as Perfecti, they were called "good men" or "friends of God". The name Perfecti come from the Latin *hereticus perfectus* ("complete heretic") used by the Inquisition, with no meaning of perfection, quite the reverse. The heretics were given various names: Cathars, Patarins, Buggers. They were also called by their place of origin: Toulousains, Agenais, Albigensians etc. but it is

Avignonet

the names Cathar and Albigensian that were most used, even far from Albi. For convenience we shall continue to use them.

Albi

BELIEF IN THE TWO PRINCIPLES

The Cathars could not accept that a single being could have conceived, on the one hand, the Kingdom of Light where Evil has no place, and on the other, the material world where Evil prospers.

Therefore there must be two basic creative principles, distinct and opposed.

God is all-powerful only for Good. His omnipotence is limited by His infinite goodness. He cannot, without inconsistency, allow Evil for He is only love. Therefore one must assume a separate principle which created the world in which Evil exists. This principle is represented by Lucifer, also known as the Prince of Darkness.

SALVATION BY KNOWLEDGE

In the beginning Satan came to lure away the followers of God. Some gave in and their souls were trapped in "tunics of flesh" and cast into the oblivion of the material world. Their minds remained with God. Salvation consists in freeing the soul from its prison of flesh and bringing it back to God and restoring the original unity of soul and mind. This re-uniting can only occur if the soul attains knowledge. Knowledge was revealed to mankind by Christ, who was sent by God for that purpose. Only baptism can bring this about. Not the baptism in water of John (for he said "another shall come and baptise you in fire and spirit") but the baptism in fire that Christ gave to His apostles, and to which the Cathars are linked by an unbroken chain. Failing this, the soul will pass to another body, waiting to attain the knowledge that brings salvation.

Montségur

Carcassonne

THE CONSOLAMENTUM

This spiritual baptism was called "consolament" in Occitan, the language of Oc, "consolamentum" in the Latin of the Inquisition. The consolamentum was only given to the believers who wished it, after three years' initiation in a house of Perfecti, or at death's door. In either case the candidate took on the rank of Perfectus. The ceremony was carried out by someone who had already attained knowledge, in the presence of other Perfecti, family and friends. After an exchange of ritual phrases and a series of prayers, the candidate was given the supreme sacrament.

The Perfecti, men and women, lived in working communities, whatever their social background. The men travelled in pairs carrying the word and doing good works in the area. Their rule was like that of the strictest monastic orders. Since an animal might contain a soul waiting for revelation, they ate no meat. Only fish, thought to be cold-blooded, was allowed. There were no sexual relations, since the creation of more "tunics of flesh" could only delay the liberation of souls.

The ordinary believer was not subject to these strict rules. He had to have faith and prepare himself to attain knowledge through the consolamentum that would be given him on his death bed. He could marry, have children, eat meat, go to war etc. When he met a Perfectus, man or woman, he would carry out the rite called in Occitan "melhorer" (improvement), mis-translated as "worship" in the documents of the Inquisition. It was a mark of respect to which the Perfectus would respond with a blessing.

THE CATHAR CHURCH

It would not appear that the Cathar churches in East and West had a common head. The Council in St Félix de Caraman in 1167 was chaired by Nicetas, an important personage from the Balkans, but that is one of the few references we have to a leading figure. On the other hand, we do know that the church was divided into dioceses, five in the Languedoc, based on Agen, Albi, Carcassonne, Toulouse (founded in St Félix de Caraman in 1167) and Razès (1226). There was another diocese in Champagne: the See of France proper. Lombardy and Tuscany had six, as did the Balkans. Each diocese was headed by a bishop, assisted by a major son and a minor son. Succession was very simple: at the death of a leader, each moved up a place and the congregation elected a new minor son. Further down the hierarchy we find deacons who were in charge of part of a diocese, and then communities of Perfecti. These workshops-cum-training centres were headed either by a prioress, for a community of women, or the oldest member, in the case of men. The mass of the faithful formed the base of Cathar society.

Penne-d'Agenais

Toulouse

THE END OF CATHARISM

The crusade called by Innocent III, which ravaged Languedoc at the start of the 13th century was intended to root out heresy from these Catholic lands and restore the unity of the Roman church. The military operations did not have the religious effects hoped for. In spite of all the assaults it faced, Catharism continued to develop. Rome then set up a new weapon of repression, an extraordinary and remarkably effective instrument, the Inquisition. Catharism in Languedoc was the first victim of interrogation, harassment, torture and execution at the stake, and gradually declined. To escape persecution the last Western Cathars fled to Northern Italy. This retreat later extended further East, when the Lombard Cathars joined the Bogomil churches. Invasion by the Turks forced the Balkan lords to seek the support of the Vatican. Dualist Christianity was repressed once more, before being finally absorbed by the Muslim Turkish occupiers in the latter half of the 15th century. It would be wrong to think that the Inquisition forced all the "heretics" into exile or conversion. Many found refuge in the large number of dissident movements which in the 16th century gave rise to the Reformation.

Villefranche-de-Lauragais

Montségur

THE CATHAR CASTLES

MONTSEGUR

The Cathars chose as their capital a spur of rock in the Ariège, 1207 m high (3960ft) on the northern face of the Saint-Barthélemy massif, overlooking the hills of Plantaurel and Lauragais beyond.

Its name is Montségur: the secure mountain.

This place with its tragic history is a symbol of a people who wanted nothing more than the right to think and live freely in the land of their ancestors.

Montségur

Montségur

THE CASTLE'S HISTORY

Rebuilt in 1204 by Raymond de Péreille at the request of the Cathars, Montségur remained throughout the period a holy place of Catharism and the symbol of resistance to the invader. The rigours of the crusades and the harshness of the Treaty of Paris did not interfere with life round the peak, or "pog" as it is called in Occitan. Pilgrims came in their hundreds. In 1232, in the face of ever greater threats, Guilhabert de Castres, head of the Cathar church, decided to withdraw to a well defended stronghold and thus protect the basic structure of Catharism. Montségur was chosen. Aware of the huge risk he was taking, Raymond de Péreille allowed his castle to become the capital of the Cathar church. It was a blatant challenge to the authority of Church and king.

It may seem surprising that the crusaders and later the Inquisition did not take more of an interest in Montségur. But the whole country was in uproar, many towns were rising up against their new masters and the maintenance of order was the first priority. It was not until 1241 that the king reminded Raymond VII of his undertaking to fight heresy. That year Louis IX asked the count to destroy the castle. Raymond brought up his troops, but a purely symbolic siege was raised after a few days. The promise made by the count of Toulouse to the King of France on 14 March 1241 makes no mention of any fortress other than this one. This suggests the crucial role played by Montségur in the religious and possibly even civilian resistance.

The defenders of Montségur were mainly concerned with escorting the Perfecti travelling along the roads of the South of France. Their first military operation was in 1242 when about sixty men-at-arms, under Pierre Roger de Mirepoix, left the castle to make their way to Avignonet. There, with local help, they slaughtered the members of the recently installed Inquisition court. This operation, intended obviously to avenge the misdeeds of the Inquisition in the South, was the act that sealed the fate of the Cathar sanctuary. For in early 1243 the Council of Béziers decided to destroy Montségur.

Montségur

THE SIEGE

During May 1243 six thousand men under Hugues des Arcis, seneschal of Carcassonne, and Pierre Amiel, archbishop of Narbonne, took up position at the foot of the outcrop. The forces were grotesquely unbalanced. The total of people living in the castle was about five hundred including the garrison of about 150 men, with fifteen knights and squires.

It is not easy to cut off a citadel of this sort. The lie of the land and the size of the outcrop need a large body of soldiers. In such conditions only the most strategic points can be under continual surveillance. Furthermore, some of the mercenaries came from neighbouring villages, in particular Camon. Men from this last place had the job of guarding part of the North-facing cliff. As a result the Northerners' blockade was less than watertight, especially since the occupants of the castle were familiar with the area. Messages, supplies and reinforcements continued to pass through the besiegers' lines.

The weeks passed and the royal army began to lose patience, with winter near and no sign of change. So Hugues des Arcis took on Gascon mercenaries who knew the mountains, and they advanced on the outcrop by night. They killed the first defenders they found and seized the tower at the Eastern end of the outcrop, on top of the cliff now known as "Tower Rock". The crusaders advanced along the ridge and within range of the castle set up a catapult under the orders of Durand, bishop of Albi. This siege engine corresponded to one built inside the castle by Bertrand de la Vacalarie, who had slipped in to help the defenders in January 1244. Casualties were many on both sides at the top of the mountain. The siege went on for another two long months, through the worst of the Pyrenean winter. Food ran short, life became harder, and when all hope of relief had gone, the defenders negotiated their surrender.

Montségur

SURRENDER AND BURNING

On Wednesday 2 March discussion began between Pierre Roger de Mirepoix, commanding the Montségur garrison, and the seneschal of Carcassonne, Hugues des Arcis. The surrender terms were relatively mild, which suggests that Pierre Roger de Mirepoix still had room for manoeuvre and that the royal army had been sorely affected by the harsh winter. The terms were roughly as follows:

- The defenders had a truce of fifteen days during which they could stay in the fortress and then hand it over to the King of France. Hostages would be taken as guarantee.

- The convictions against a number of defenders were waived. There was an amnesty for the men who took part in the raid on Avignonet.

- The soldiers would be free to leave after appearing before the Inquisition.
- Any other person living in the castle or the village would also be free, if they gave up their Cathar faith, after making their statement to the Inquisition. The rest would be burnt at the stake.

It is not clear why Pierre Roger asked for a fifteen day truce; perhaps he still expected relief. Possibly the defenders wanted this period to put their affairs in order. We do know that the Cathars used the truce to prepare themselves spiritually for death and to give away all their worldly goods to the soldiers who had lived beside them for ten months. We also know that some people, including soldiers, converted to Catharism in full knowledge of the fate that awaited them.

Montségur

On the morning of 16 March the archbishop of Narbonne and the seneschal of Carcassonne came to take possession. The lord of the manor, Raymond de Péreille, and his son-in-law, Pierre Roger de Mirepoix, in charge of the garrison, handed the castle over. For their part the Cathars were ready. Led by Bertrand Marty, their bishop, they walked bravely down the mountainside. At the bottom there was a stockade filled with firewood. Climbing ladders up the side the Perfecti hurled themselves into the flames, while the injured were thrown with their stretchers into the stockade. In this way perished 225 men and women.

The holy place of Catharism, the symbol of resistance, had fallen. Forty years of history, ten months of siege, 225 martyrs in the flames, ensure for Montségur a place in legend.

THE TREASURE

Not all the Perfecti were burnt that 16 March. At the request of Bertrand Marty, four of them were hidden by Pierre Roger de Mirepoix in a crack in the rock. During the night of the 15th they were lowered by rope down the cliff. Leaving Montségur and crossing the pass of La Peyre they made their way to a cave on the other side where they recovered the "treasure" which two other Perfecti had stowed away three months earlier, around Christmas. Via Caussou and Montaillou they went to the castle of Usson where they were joined by one of the two heretics who had hidden the precious burden. Then all trace of them disappears.

The treasure of Montségur - since its existence was first mentioned, the casket hidden by two Perfecti in a cave in Sabarthès has turned into a fabulous treasure of gold coin,

Montségur

Montségur

precious stones, sacred texts, or even the Holy Grail. The reality was probably quite different. There must have been coins, for we know that the Cathar communities in Lombardy received sums of money for their needs. Much later, in Northern Italy, there are signs of one of the four fugitives. But it is doubtful if money was the only reason for their escape. The treasure they recovered shortly after their comrades were burnt must have been very important for them to break the terms of surrender, contrary to their integrity. Furthermore this action would have put Pierre Roger de Mirepoix in a difficult position, had it been discovered. The mild terms he had obtained in early March would certainly not have been maintained. From that point of view, hiding money cannot have been the sole purpose of their action. At that time manuscripts were rare and expensive. The Cathars had texts in the "vulgar tongue", i.e. Occitan, which could be widely understood. It is easy to suppose that in such conditions the Cathar church wanted to ensure the safety of manuscripts concerned with dogma or ritual. Perhaps that was the treasure.

Montségur

is a small opening, on the right steps to the ramparts, and on the left rises the keep with two bays. There are also signs of building work. The walls have regularly placed square holes for beams. Sections of wall barely emerging from the ground suggest foundations. The courtyard had lean-to sheds against the walls and a triangular shaft for light in the middle.

Less clear is how five hundred people lived here during the siege. Most of the garrison must have been quartered within the walls, where weapons and food were kept. The other defenders had built a sort of small village at the foot of the fortress. Evidence of habitation has been found on the Northern and Western sides of the outcrop. The village was most probably defended by a wooden stockade. The lord of the manor, Raymond de Péreille, and his son-in-law Pierre Roger de Mirepoix, will have lived with their family in the keep. The main entrance to the keep was in the courtyard at first-floor level. Access was by a moveable gangway between the ramparts and a balcony of which traces can still be seen below the doorway. Nowadays the keep is entered by a wide breach in the Western wall. The first room you come to was a water-tank, and beyond the second wall you find the lower chamber, where the vaulting has now collapsed. Originally this chamber could only be reached from the first floor via the spiral staircase whose marks can be seen at the far end on the right.

Although the setting is impressive and attractive, it is the building itself that is a source of curiosity for the visitor. After a 20 or 30 minute climb you walk into a small courtyard of some 700 sq m (7500 sq ft), surrounded by high walls. Opposite the main entrance

Montségur

MILITARY DEFENCES

The castle's natural defences are considerable. The cliffs of the outcrop are steep and high. But fortification is also necessary. The South-West flank, easiest of access, was protected by three walls. There was a watchpost set up at the Eastern end of the outcrop, at the top of Tower Rock. The village below the castle walls was surrounded by a wooden stockade with a barbican (double gate) to the East. The approach along the ridge is broken at the foot of the citadel. The break is in fact a quarry which provided the stones for the castle. The quarry was dug here both because it was near to the building work and as part of the defences.

The walls along the top of the mountain are the final rampart. The surprisingly large Southern gate was defended by an overhanging wooden gallery attached to the top of the wall. Movable wooden platforms were used to reach the bottom of the opening. The battlement walkway could be reached by three stairways. The Eastern wall has been reinforced to a width of over four metres (14ft). Deep slots can be seen which held beams projecting outwards and supported by diagonal beams resting on studs still visible. This provided a wide fortified platform which could take a catapult if necessary.

THE SUMMER SOLSTICE AT MONTSEGUR

The castle is built on such a strange plan that close study has led to the most unusual theories. First of all, the building is oriented towards the four points of the compass (see upper diagram). The most striking alignment occurs on the morning of the summer solstice. At sunrise that day the first rays of sunlight enter the East-facing arrow-slits in the lower chamber of the keep and leave by the West-facing ones. As the sun moves on, it marks out through these narrow openings two rectangles of light that move across the inner sides of the slits opposite. Then they disappear and finally light up the walls of the chamber.

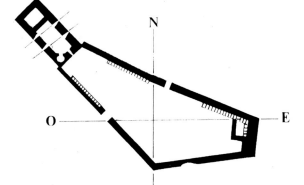

These strange features have caused some people to claim that the castle was a solar temple. We merely record these features without giving them any special interpretation. Any connexion between Catharism and some sort of sun worship is quite impossible, and such architectural oddities can be explained by the traditions of master builders. Furthermore the building we see today cannot be precisely as it was when Raymond de Péreille rebuilt it in 1204 at the request of the Cathars. After the siege in 1244, Montségur was given to the Lévis family to whom Simon de Montfort had allotted it right at the start of the crusade. After that the castle held a garrison for a long time and necessarily underwent a number of changes.

Alignment on the morning of the summer solstice

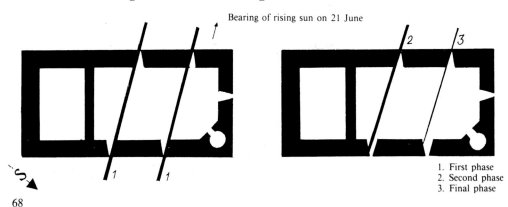

Bearing of rising sun on 21 June

1. First phase
2. Second phase
3. Final phase

AGUILAR

To the East of Tuchan, not far from the road North from Estagel to Narbonne, impressive ruins can be seen on a hill 300 m (1000 ft) high. This is the castle of Aguilar overlooking a dry landscape of vineyards and scrubland.

West of the entrance beside the old path stands a little chapel dedicated to Saint Anne. Its tiny oblong nave under a barrel vault opens out on to a slightly raised apse. As you enter the castle itself you can see to the right of the entrance a sentry-box let into the thickness of the wall under a stairway leading to the battlements. Here was the jousting ground between the inner and outer walls. The outer wall, hexagonal in shape, has an open tower at each angle equipped with arrow-slits on two levels. In the North-East and South-West corners stairways led to the ramparts. The inner wall, which must be the original castle, stands on the highest part of the hill. The walls with their vaulted arrow-slits enclose a yard of roughly 350 sq m area (3700 sq ft). On the Northern wall is the keep, a rectangular tower rising on two levels above a basement water-tank.

No documents have yet been found to date the building of the castle. Belonging to the county of Barcelona, it was entrusted to the lords of Termes, subject to the Trencavels, themselves under the counts of Barcelona, kings of Aragon. No doubt linked to the fate of the castle of Termes, Aguilar went through the Albigensian period without playing an important role. But when the French crown had annexed the lands of the Trencavels and set about defending them against Aragon, Aguilar together with Puilaurens, Peyrepertuse, Quéribus and Termes made up the "five sons of Carcassonne", the name given to the fortresses defending that town. Aguilar was garrisoned until the late 16th century and then abandoned.

ARQUES

Not much is left of the castle first mentioned in the mid-12th century. It consisted of a large oblong enclosure, of which only the Southern part remains. As you pass under a gothic arch and the arms of the de Voisins family you enter what was the courtyard. The South-West corner is fortified with a square tower. In the centre is a remarkably well preserved square keep. Its width is 11 m (36 ft) and height about 25 m (80 ft). The corners carry round watch-towers. During the Albigensian crusade the castle was given to Pierre de Voisins, a companion of Simon de Montfort, for services rendered on the crusade. Later it passed to the de Joyeuse family.

CARCASSONNE

"Not to my knowledge is there anywhere else in Europe so complete and impressive a defensive system". After his restoration work Viollet-le-Duc could have added "or anywhere in the world", for this medieval walled city is unique.

A small Gaulish village was succeeded by a fortified Roman town covering probably the area of the present inner walls. Next the Visigoths in the 5th and 6th centuries AD, then the Arabs from 725 to 759 realised the advantages of the town's position. The great building works of the Middle Ages were ordered by the Trencavel dynasty. They built the castle of the counts in 1130 and some years later St Nazaire cathedral.

Then came the dark years of the Albigensian crusade. Besieged in the walled city in July 1209, Raymond Roger de Trencavel had to face the attacks of the crusaders, only a week after the sack of Béziers. The lack of food and water forced the viscount to negotiate. Betrayed and imprisoned, he was murdered a few weeks later. Taking the title of viscount of Béziers and Carcassonne, Simon de Montfort made the city the headquarters of his crusade. In 1229 the viscountcy was abolished; the territory was annexed by the French crown, made a seneschalcy and administered by crown agents.

The younger Raymond Trencavel, leading an army raised in the Corbières, tried in 1240 to recover the family lands. Outflanked by the royal army and forced to lift the siege when he was about to take the city, Trencavel returned once more to exile.

After this experience, which showed up certain weaknesses in the defences, the city was turned into an impregnable fortress. The inner walls were restored and topped with twenty-eight towers, outer walls were added with thirteen more towers, and all routes of access remarkably defended. From then on the walled city's function was essentially military, and the civilian population moved in about 1260 down to the present town. Carcassonne became the headquarters of a defensive system directed towards Catalonia. Aguilar, Puilaurens, Quéribus, Peyrepertuse and Termes were its main outposts; they were called the "five sons" of Carcassonne.

In 1659 the Treaty of the Pyrenees ceding Roussillon to the French crown removed much of Carcassonne's strategic importance, since the border was moved South. The city became no more than an arms depot and barracks, and gradually the defences were left to rot. In the early 19th century the Army as owner turned the walled city into a vast quarry and sold off the stones. Prosper Mérimée in 1835 was the first to protest. Twenty years later Viollet-le-Duc undertook the extensive restoration work. This 19th century work did not always respect the original architecture, but we should still thank Viollet-le-Duc, for without his perseverence the walled city would not exist today.

COUSTAUSSA

Seen from the road from Couiza into the Corbières via the Paradis pass, the ruins of the castle of Coustaussa are most impressive. For all their noble airs, it is only a few sections of wall that face the valley. The castle was built by the Trencavels in the mid-12th century and occupied by Simon de Montfort in 1210 when it was abandoned. The following year it was besieged by the crusaders and surrendered after only a few days. Coustaussa was inhabited until the early 19th century, when it was largely pulled down.

FOIX

The huge rock rising above the confluence of the Ariège and the Arget is obviously the perfect place from which to command the trade routes along the two rivers. Looking North to the Pas de la Barre and South up the valley of the Ariège as far as Andorra and the road to Spain, the location cries out for fortification. Some work was carried out in 1002 AD by the first count of Foix, Roger-Bernard, younger son of Roger the Elder, count of Carcassonne. Till that date the lords of the country round Foix were the abbots of Saint-Volusien, subject to the counts of Carcassonne. The building is not mentioned in texts before the middle of the 13th century, when the seal of Roger IV of Foix (1241-1265) shows that the castle already had two square towers with battlements, joined by a domestic building. The round tower to the South was not built until the 15th century. More than 34 metres high (112 ft) and built on a steep slope, it is supported by an impressive flying buttress. Close study of the site shows that it was defended by two walls with a large barbican (double gate). The town lay at the foot of the rock, protected by ramparts joining the natural defences of the two rivers. These walls ran along the line of the present Allées de Villote.

The alliance between Foix and Béarn in the early 14th century removed from the fortress the role of sole capital, since the lords of Foix spent their time elsewhere too.

The castle remained a feudal residence until the end of the 16th century, when it became purely military in function. Its strategic position on the road to Spain spared it the destructions orderd by Cardinal Richelieu. In the early 18th century the Provincial government occupied the building, but a few years later the Revolution turned it into a prison. Napoleon gave it to the département in 1811. A plan to restore its defensive function was soon dropped and the castle sank into oblivion. Only in 1886 was restoration work begun. Sheds and hovels which had cluttered it up for decades were removed and the castle buildings restored and strengthened. The work was carried out by a pupil of Viollet-le-Duc, Paul Boewilwald. Once more the castle deserved the adjective "fantastic" given it by the historian Michelet.

The counts of Foix were never ordained Perfecti, but many members of their family, including even wives and sisters, received the consolamentum. But family reasons alone cannot explain the efforts of the county of Foix in the resistance to the Albigensian crusades; the counts were quick to defend not only their people but also their rights. They proved this many times, as Simon de Montfort learnt to his cost, especially at the battles of Montgey and Saint-Martin-Lalande. The military skills of the lords of Foix were such that Montfort failed in every attempt to take the castle. By a diplomatic manoeuvre at the Lateran Council in 1215 he managed to install a Northern French garrison, but Raymond-Roger soon recovered his property.

LASTOURS

A few kilometres North of Carcassonne two streams from the Black Mountain, the Orbiel and the Greisillon have cut deeply into the rock and formed at their confluence an impressive massif with four peaks, each topped by the remains of a castle. This is Lastours. You reach the ruins up a path from the banks of the Orbiel. As you stand on the plateau to the West of the village you see all four at once. To the left, Cabaret the most impressive and oldest, first mentioned in 1063. There lived the lord and the famous Louve de Pennautier and her gallant troubadour Raymond de Miraval. A few metres higher rises Tour Régine, just a tower and a modest enclosing wall. This building is the most recent, dating from after the crusade. At first it was naturally called Tour Neuve (new tower), but then Tour Régine, or royal tower, clearly indicating who ordered its construction. First mentioned in 1260. Further to the right at the end of the ridge stands Fleur Espine or Surespine, a square keep guarding a small courtyard enclosed by a wall since pulled down. This castle was built in the first half of the 12th century. Fourth and last, Quertinheux stands on a spur of rock in the foreground.

LORDAT

The impressive rock that rises 400 m (1300 ft) above the River Ariège upstream from Tarascon is of great strategic significance. The castle of Lordat at the top commands the valley and the roads from Foix to Catalonia via the Puymaurens pass, to the Pays de Soult via Marmare, and to Quérigut via Pailhères. This position must have been used since earliest times, but the first mention is not until the 10th century, when Roger the Elder, count of Carcassonne, granted various lands including Vèbre in the Lordat area to someone called Sanche. During the 11th century the castle was a source of dispute between the counts of Foix and Cerdagne, each claiming the area. But it appears that when Roger the Elder's estates were divided, Lordat fell to the younger son, Roger-Bernard, first count of Foix. The Albigensian crusade spared the castle, although it often gave shelter to Cathar Perfecti including Guilhabert de Castres in 1224. On 16 June 1229 Roger-Bernard II, count of Foix, submitting to the Church and the French king in the church of Saint-Jean-de-Verges, handed over as pledges the castles of Lordat and Montgrenier, which were only returned to him five years later. Rebuilt in the 14th century, Lordat's role in the history of the county of Foix was more diplomatic than military. After bloody events in the area during the Wars of Religion (16th century) the King of Navarre,

later Henri IV, ordered the destruction of the castle, but rescinded the order after an inquiry. Although it survived Cardinal Richelieu's destruction policy, the castle fell into disuse and was then abandoned to the elements.

The oval shape of the castle follows the lines of the outcrop. The walls enclose an area nearly 100 m by 50 m (108 by 54 yards). A series of three walls on the easiest slope join to form a single defensive wall on the steepest side. They form a striking system of defences around the keep, of which only sections of wall are left.

MIGLOS

On a spur of rock not far from the prehistoric cave at Niaux, the castle of Miglos commands the valley of the Vicdessos stream from its confluence with the Ariège to Vicdessos village.

The square fortress contains in its Eastern corner an oblong keep some 20 m high (65 ft). In the opposite corner is another oblong structure with a vaulted water-tank on the ground floor. Various buildings join the two towers, forming a small inner courtyard. The East wall, overlooking the path from Baychon, has angled arrow-slits pointing at different points on the path.

First mentioned in the mid-12th century, the castle was the seat of the barony of Miglos, subject to the counts of Foix. The existing village covers the territory of the barony, including the hamlets of Arquizat, Axiat, Baychon, Norgeat and Norrat. In the early 14th century the castle passed from the Miglos to the Usson family. On 10 November 1320, the new lord agreed with his tenants the fines to be paid by them for not working on the upkeep of the castle. Miglos soon lost its military importance and became a residence, changing hands several times. The last owners were turned out during the French Revolution, leaving the place a ruin.

MINERVE

North of Lézignan a section of the limestone plateau has been cut into the form of a shinbone by the two streams called Cesse and, rather improbably, Brian. Although the streams are often dry, the gorges they have dug are so deep as to be marvellous natural defences. On the narrowest part of the "bone" the

lords of Minerve built their castle, guarding access to the walled village at the round end. On either side of the castle there were moats with drawbridges, allowing the fortress to be cut off both from the plateau and the village. Only a stone obelisk remains of the keep which formed an impressive shield along the only level access. Rising from the sheer cliffs, ramparts with towers enclosed the settlement, with two gates allowing access. A narrow fortified stairway led down to a small covered well near the confluence.

Guided by Aimery de Narbonne, sworn enemy of viscount Guillaume of Minerve, Simon de Montfort laid siege to Minerve on 15 June 1210. Soon realising that water was the fortress's weak spot, Montfort aimed the most powerful of his four catapults at the stairway down to the well. Once the access to the well was destroyed, Minerve had no water, and after a five week siege the Viscount was forced to sue for terms. Confident of their superiority the crusaders refused to negotiate, forcing Guillaume of Minerve to surrender unconditionally, and Montfort took the castle. On 22 July 140 Perfecti, men and women, were thrown to the flames of a huge pyre. A garrison of Northern troops was installed and the occupation lasted while the castle was of any strategic importance. It was later abandoned and became a hide-out for highwaymen until Louis XIII ordered its destruction in 1637.

MONTAILLOU

East of the Ariège Pyrenees, the Pays d'Aillon runs along the foothills and up to the Chioula pass. On this plateau is a hillock, the Mont d'Aillon, which gave its name both to the castle and the village on the slope. That name is Montaillou, famous for the twenty-five hearings conducted by the bishop-inquisitor Jacques Fournier from 1318 to 1325. After studying the records of the Pamiers Inquisition, Emmanuel Le Roi Ladurie published his book "Montaillou".

Only a few sections of wall are left of the castle. Although the castle was untouched by the Albigensian crusades, the local area was deeply involved in the heresy. Some of the villagers were in touch with nearby Montségur, and at the end of the 13th century the Authié brothers, Cathar Perfecti, had a small congregation here.

Since the Pays d'Aillon came directly under the county of Foix, the castle was the seat of feudal authority, in the shape of two men: the lord of the manor, in charge of army and police matters, and the bailiff, who delivered justice in the count's name and collected taxes.

PEYREPERTUSE

North-East of the Galamus gorges in the Corbières a huge barrier of rock runs East to West. Rising to 800 m (2500 ft) it is 300 m long and more than 50 m at the widest point (330 by 60 yards). The South cliff conceals a cave, and to the North there is a shelter beneath the rock. These openings may once have been connected, giving the name "pierced rock", Peyrepertuse, modern French "pierre percée". The top of the rock was put entirely to military use. First the flatter Eastern end, where solid walls with open towers joined by a walkway were built over the sheer cliff face. Opposite the entrance, defended by a zigzag passage, can be seen the well restored remains of the original castle and the Chapel of Sainte-Marie (1115). In the middle of the enclosure is a vast esplanade commanded by the ruins of the castle of Saint-Jordy to the East, built on the orders of Louis IX in 1242. It can be reached by the so-called stairway of Saint Louis, a hundred or so steps cut into the rock.

In the 9th century Peyrepertuse belonged to the county of Bésalu. Two centuries later it came under the authority of the counts of Barcelona, later to become kings of Aragon. Despite its size and position the castle played only a minor role in the Albigensian crusade. In autumn 1240 Trencavel was forced to raise the siege of Carcassonne and seek refuge in Peyrepertuse. The Northern French troops at his heels laid siege to the castle. Caught without supplies, the castle surrendered on 16 November after only three days. The Treaty of Corbeil in 1258, settling the details of the borders with Catalonia, gave the castle to the King of France. With a royal garrison it became an important part of the defensive system based on Carcassonne. When Roussillon was annexed by France in 1659, the castle lost its strategic importance and sank into oblivion.

PUILAURENS

Commanding the road up the River Boulzane from the Aude valley to Conflent, the castle of Puilaurens stands on an outcrop of rock not far from the gorges of Pierre-Lys. The only access is by a zigzag path up a narrow natural corridor. The keep at the Western end overlooks the path up to a large gateway. This leads into a chamber with twelve arrow-slits in the walls, all aimed at the doorway. Beyond this final defence is a large courtyard enclosed by battlemented walls with a walkway. The walls follow the irregular shape of the rock. There are remains of a storehouse or living quarters in the middle of the yard.

The castle itself is reached by a narrow path above the main entrance.

Puilaurens is first mentioned in documents of the late 10th century. It belonged to the Fenouillet family, subject to the count of Bésalu. Then it came under the counts of Barcelona, then the kings of Aragon. On the death of viscount Pierre de Fenouillet in 1243, his lieutenant Chabert de Barbaira took over the castle until 1256. Then he was kidnapped and gave the castle away as a ransom, together with Quéribus. With the Treaty of Corbeil in 1258 it passed into the hands of the King of France, but the royal garrison was withdrawn, as in so many places, when in 1659 the Treaty of the Pyrenees moved the frontier further South.

PUIVERT

In a large natural basin between Lavelanet and Quillan rise the gentle slopes of a hill on which stands the castle of Puivert. Quite unlike the other fortresses of the area, there are no sheer cliffs and it is easy to approach. A wide open space leads up to the Eastern frontage, the corners defended by two round towers, one of which has now collapsed. You pass through a gatehouse with the arms of the Bruyère family into the courtyard. A drawbridge once crossed a moat which has now been mostly filled in. The huge space before you is enclosed by walls with a battlement walkway. To the left the "Tour Gaillarde" is all that remains of a building that collapsed in the early 19th century. To the right the enclosing wall and round tower with masonry bosses are much better preserved. And at the far end stands the square keep, 15 m wide (50 ft) and more than 30 m high (100 ft). The two lower floors, partly below ground, have round vaulting. The third level is entered through a pointed archway with shields bearing the arms of the Bruyère and Melun families. Once the chapel, this chamber has rib vaulting. The six ribs join in a keystone representing God the Father and a praying Virgin. The other ends rest on supports in the form of figures with scrolls. The upper chamber is called the "Musician's Hall" because of the carvings on the eight supports of the vaulting, musicians with their instruments, while the keystone bears the Bruyère arms. The fifth level is a terrace that was once battlemented. This building dates from the 14th century; the old ruined castle behind the keep is 13th century.

The castle of Puivert belonged to the Congost family, the head of which, Bernard, married Alpaïs, sister of Raymond de Péreille, who was lord of Montségur. After a three day siege the castle surrendered to the crusaders in autumn 1210 and Simon de Montfort gave it to Lambert de Thury. Later it belonged to Thomas Pons de Bruyère who made alterations in the 14th century. The twin shields over the door to the third level represent his marriage to Isabeau de Melun in 1310.

QUERIBUS

Perched stockily on its summit, the castle of Quéribus commands the Grau de Maury, the pass linking the villages of Maury and Cucugnan. The curé of Cucugnan in Alphonse Daudet's "Letters from My Mill" came, therefore, from Languedoc rather than Provence, and must have said mass in the chapel of Saint-Louis-de-Quéribus.

You enter the enclosure via a zigzag passage and a gateway. The gun emplacements defending the entrance prove that the fortress was used until a late period. After the gateway there is a narrow stairway up the side of the cliff, past remnants of the defences, to the castle itself. You walk through some dilapidated buildings, and across a tiny court-yard you see the impressive mass of the keep, a polygonal tower. The walls are so thick they contain a

secret room from which a passage leads through rock and stonework to a blockhouse on the cliff. The main hall of the keep, reached by a spiral staircase, has ribbed vaulting with a splendid off-centre round pillar. The use of this hall is far from clear, because of the various windows, different levels, remains of a fireplace, off-centre pillar. Most probably it was the chapel of Saint-Louis-de-Quéribus, restored in the early 15th century.

Quéribus is first mentioned in a document in the early 11th century. Subject to the count of Bésalu, like most of the castles in the area it was attached first to the county of Barcelona, then the kingdom of Aragon and finally the kingdom of France by the Treaty of Corbeil in 1258. It was then a true frontier castle, for the natural border was

the line of cliffs on which it was built. The Treaty of the Pyrenees in 1659, moving the frontier South, took away its strategic importance. A document of 1689 states that the priest in Cucugnan was also chaplain to the castle garrison, and in charge of ministering to the soldiers and civilians in Quéribus, saying mass there on the feast-day of St Louis.

ROQUEFIXADE

Half-way along the road between Foix and Lavelanet, a rugged cliff stands out against the sky. Unless you know what to look for, it is hard to make out the remains of the fortress of Roquefixade in the shape of the rock. This stronghold commanded the road West from Foix to the Pays d'Olmes. You make your way first along the cliff and then turn sharply upwards across a steep meadow. To the right a deep cleft in the the sheer rockface is spanned by part of the castle wall. This fissure in the rock must be the origin of the name Roquefixade. The path leads you on to a wide space that must have been the castle courtyard. The castle itself was built on the highest point of the rock, and is entered through a gatehouse where you can see above you signs of a hole for dropping heavy objects on attackers. Unfortunately very little of the building is left, but you can just make out where the keep stood, at the point where the enclosing wall spans the cleft.

Part of the defences of the Pays d'Olmes, Roquefixade was subject to the counts of Toulouse who had passed their rights over the castle to the counts of Foix. These rights were taken back during a quarrel between the two families in February 1243. After the Albigensian crusade Roquefixade passed to the French crown and a Northern garrison was installed, twelve sergeants, a porter, a watchman and a chaplain. On 28 October 1632 Louis XIII, who had come to watch the execution of the Duc de Montmorency in Toulouse, ordered the castle of Roquefixade to be destroyed. The following year his instructions were carried out, unfortunately to the letter.

TERMES

It is hard today as you stand amid the lonely ruins of the castle to imagine the splendour of the lords of Termes. For many years they fought the abbey of Lagrasse for possession of the Corbières, especially the mines. It was from mining rather than farming that the lords of Termes gained their wealth and power. In the heart of the Corbières, on a plateau surrounded on three sides by the gorges of the little river Sou, a tributary of the Orbieu, stand the ruins of the castle of Termes. Among the dismantled walls you can just make out the shape of the original building. There were two enclosures separated by a jousting ground. In the middle stood the castle and keep. Little remains of the huge building: a section of wall with a strange cross-shaped window, a buttress which must have supported a corner tower near the Northern gate, channels running down inside the Western wall, emerging behind two round arches, possibly a defensive structure, but more likely the outlets from the latrines above.

Termes is first mentioned in 1110. During the Albigensian crusade the castle belonged to Raymond de Termes, a powerful subject of the viscounts of Carcassonne. An old man, Raymond was fiercely opposed to the invasion of the crusading army. A large part of that army laid siege to his castle and he only surrendered after four months, beaten more by hunger and thirst than the valour of the besiegers. On 23 November 1210 Simon de Montfort put one of his companions, Alain de Roucy, into the castle he had fought so hard to take. In 1224 the defeated Amaury de Montfort gave it to the archbishop of Narbonne. Five years later Termes passed to the French crown. A lord of the manor and a garrison of twelve men-at-arms occupied it for four centuries until it lost its strategic importance and was abandoned. Highwaymen used it next and the king ordered its destruction. It was blown up in 1653.

USSON

At the confluence of the rivers Aude and Bruyante, on a rock cliff, stand the remnants of the walls of the castle of Usson. The castle once commanded the valleys leading to Roussillon and Donezan. The building is now in an appalling state of ruin, crumbling and overgrown. Among the mass of stones it is easy to pick out the elaborate defensive system and access to the gateway.

The gun emplacements in the walls show that the castle was extensively rebuilt, the alterations occurring in the 17th and 18th centuries.

First mention of the castle goes back to the early 11th century when it belonged to the Alion family. They were deeply involved with the Cathar movement, and even at the most difficult times for Montségur, relations between the two castles were maintained. After the executions on 16 March 1244 the four Perfecti who had recovered the "treasure of Montségur" came to Usson to meet Mathieu, one of the two Perfecti who had hidden it some weeks earlier. The Pays du Donezan passed to the French crown in the 17th century. Louis XIII put a lord of the manor and a small garrison into the castle of Usson, but in 1711 Louis XIV sold the fortress to a descendant of the Usson family who made extensive alterations. It was confiscated during the French Revolution and sold off as public property. Later it was plundered for building materials by the uncultured locals.

VILLEROUGE-TERMENES

Former summer residence of the archbishops of Narbonne, Ville-rouge-Termenès was virtually untouched by the Albigensian crusade. On 24 August 1321 Bélibaste, the last Perfectus in Languedoc, was burnt at the stake here. Now the castle is set in the village, or rather the village has grown up round the castle. This may be why the basic building has been preserved. The four corners of the enclosing wall were guarded by towers, and the South-East one, the most impressive, was the keep.

MEDIEVAL MANUSCRIPT SOURCES

For decades the mysteries of Catharism have been maintained by many and varied books dealing in controversy, not to mention propaganda.

A large number of documents have been discovered and catalogued to date. Most have been studied and translated, some even published. Catharism is no longer a nebulous mystery; there is plenty of written evidence to support both serious historical research and excellent books intended for a wider audience.

Here is a selection of the major medieval manuscripts:

Hearings by the Inquisitor Bernard de Caux of the brothers Jourdain and Aribert, co-lords of Mas-Saintes-Puelles.

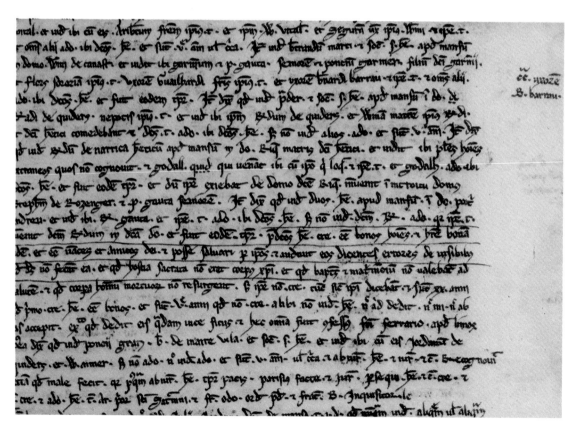

Contemporary accounts

- *The Song of the Albigensian Crusade*, a chronicle by Guillaume de Tudèle and an anonymous author. Occitan manuscript in the Bibliothèque Nationale in Paris.
- *The Chronicle of Guillaume de Puylaurens.*
- *The Chronicle of Pierre des Vaux de Cerna.*

Cathar religious documents

- *The Lyon Ritual.* The New Testament followed by a Cathar liturgy written in Occitan in the 13th century.
- *The Florence Manuscript.* Latin manuscript on dogma based on the Book of the Two Principles by the Perfectus Jean de Lugio.
- *The Prague Manuscript.* Latin manuscript, copy of a treatise written in Languedoc in the early 13th century.

Anti-Cathar documents

- *The Liber contra Manicheos* by Durand de Huesca.
- *The Summa quadripartita* by Alain de Lille.

Judicial documents

Not all these many sources have yet been fully examined. One of the better known documents is The Register of the Inquisition of Jacques Fournier. In this register are all the hearings of the inquisitorial tribunal in Pamiers in the early 14th century under the future Benedict XII.

Copies of all the medieval Cathar archives found to date are kept in the Centre René Nelli, Centre National d'Etudes Cathares, at Villegly near Carcassonne.

Rituel cathare.

FURTHER READING

In French :

Cathar life :
René NELLI :
La vie quotidienne des cathares du Languedoc au XIII° siècle,
Hachette, 1969.

Religion :
Edina BOZOKY
Le livre secret des cathares,
Beauchesne, 1980.
Anne BRENON
Le vrai visage du catharisme,
NOTRE HISTOIRE 1990 prize.
Loubatières, 1988.
Jean DUVERNOY
Le catharisme.
T 1 - *La religion des cathares,*
Privat, 1976.
T 2 - *L'histoire des cathares,*
Privat, 1979.

History :
Jacques MADAULE
Le drame albigeois et l'unité française,
Gallimard, 1973.
Zoé OLDENBOURG
Le bûcher de Montségur,
Gallimard, 1959.

Michel ROQUEBERT
L'épopée cathare,
Privat, 1970-1977-1986-1989.
Aymeric et les cathares :
comic book,
illustrated by G. Forton,
Loubatières, 1978.
Aymeric à Montségur :
comic book,
illustrated by G. Forton,
Loubatières, 1981.

In English :

Bernard HAMILTON
The Albigensian Crusade Historical Association, London, 1974.
Emmanuel LE ROI LADURIE
Montaillou: Cathars and Catholics in a French village 1294 - 1324 Penguin, 1978.
Zoë OLDENBOURG
Massacre at Montsegur
Weidenfeld & Nicolson, 1961.
Jonathan SUMPTION
The Albigensian Crusade
Faber & Faber, 1978.

The author
A devotee of Cathar history, Georges SERRUS lives at the foot of the Montségur peak or "pog". He runs the "Occitadelle", a restaurant-cum-art gallery where he puts on regular exhibitions, and a bookshop with a range of books on Catharism.
In his house he gives talks and slide-shows on all the Cathar castles.

Photographic crédits : Albarel : p. 14 — Archives départementales de la Haute-Garonne : p. 28 — Archives municipales de Toulouse : p. 28 — Audimage : p. 24, 72 — Bertrand : p. 12 — Bibliothèque municipale de Lyon : p. 93 — Bibliothèque municipale de Toulouse : p. 92 — Fauré : p. 73 — Gasc : p. 36, 46, 50, 64 — Hilaire : p. 23 — Jarlan : p. 66, 67, 69, 78, 84, 87, 88, 91 — Lasseube : p. 10, 32, 38, 55, 62, 85, 92 — Loubatières : p. 11, 13, 18, 19, 21, 22, 29, 31, 33, 35, 42, 71, 79 — Marty : p. 52 — Mayans : p. 8, 39 — Meauxonne : p. 34, 56, 59, 63 — Pons : p. 17, 74, 81, 83, 86, 87 — Roquebert : p. 3, 4, 15 — Rousseau : p. 43 — Serrus : p. 80, 90 — Sierpinski : p. 10, 16, 27, 40, 45, 49, 51, 61, 70, 76, 77, 89, 95 — Theulé : p. 50 — Vaugeois : p. 65.

Minerve

CONTENTS

© Editions Loubatières
Achevé d'imprimer sur les presses des Imprimeries Fournié,
à Fonsegrives 31130 Balma/Toulouse en juillet 1990.
Dépôt légal 3ᵉ trimestre 1990 — ISBN 2-86266-143-0